Min Tanya Pauline has penned an imaginative, creative, and humorous poetic rendition of this very familiar story of Queen Esther. Yet in her telling she remains Biblically sound and true to the original text. With each lyrical verse the reader is drawn into the story, as the story is told in the vernacular of our times. You will be pulled along in this emotional tale that speaks of the sovereignty of God and his redeeming grace! You may also discover some overlooked details of the story of Esther here illuminated by this gifted and talented Ecclesiastical raconteur! An added bonus is the eleven life lessons gleaned from this ancient story. I recommend this book as an aide to any study of the Book of Esther and to Sunday school educators seeking fresh and engaging curricula that make Bible stories relevant and relatable.

Joseph Robinson Jr., Senior Deacon
Author, 7 Leadership Imperatives from a Wild Man (Judson Press, 2008)
President, Martin Luther King Jr. Leadership Development Institute

Tanya Pauline makes this epic Bible story more palatable for all ages with rhythm and rhyme. This book is delectably creative in its use of poetry that places Esther front and center with the fairy tale princesses that little (and big girls like me) have tried to emulate over the years. It made me smile in so many places because it reminded me of all the precious lessons I have learned from Queen Esther. You'll curl up with this book or read it to your little ones time and time again.

Shari A. Loveday, M.A., LGMFT
Author of He Already Put a Ring on It, Come to Me First, and Just BeTween Us

In this book Tanya Parker does the very important work of re-enlivening an ancient, sacred text with her own voice. Though I have read the book of Esther many times, I have never experienced it with such rhythm, wit, and craft, as well as deep moral thinking woven through the narrative and the lessons afterward. As we say in the Jewish community, may Tanya "continue with strength" enlivening more ancient texts with her skilled hand.

Rabbi Ariana Capptauber
Beth El Temple, Harrisburg, PA

Esther

A Story of Rhythm, Rhyme and Truth

TANYA PAULINE

WESTBOW
PRESS®
A DIVISION OF THOMAS NELSON
& ZONDERVAN

WestBow Press books may be ordered through booksellers or by contacting:

WestBow Press
A Division of Thomas Nelson & Zondervan
1663 Liberty Drive
Bloomington, IN 47403
www.westbowpress.com
844-714-3454

Illustrations by Patricia Gordan-Rivera.

ISBN: 978-1-6642-6921-7 (sc)
ISBN: 978-1-6642-6922-4 (e)

Library of Congress Control Number: 2022911166

Print information available on the last page.

WestBow Press rev. date: 10/20/2022

This is dedicated to ALL my "grand-honeys"
(As Charley, with whom I share a few, would say)
Makayla, Michael, Sebastian, Christian,
Julia, Joshua, Jana
Liyanna,
Isaiah, Lailah, Landry
and Sky
(a few grand-nieces and nephews: Theo and Elica, Mya and Jeremiah, Jr.)
Along with James, Kevin, and Keyonna
(Book took so long you are all grown now)
Along with all I call "family."
With God's grace and creative power, more to come.

Contents

Acknowledgements

First and foremost, to my God and my friend!
Second, to my mother whose undying love
pushes me to heights unknown
and
To Marla whose tireless efforts and expert
typing skills made this possible;
To Nia and Lillian and Marla whose unswerving faith,
confidence and cheerleading made this possible;
To my "step-children"
Eugene Jr., Shanni, and Nikki who surprisingly still call me "family;"
and
(Special thanks to Shari and Nikki who lit a fire under me by being first);
and
to a host, too numerous to count, of people whose positive
accolades, strong encouragement, and unwavering faith,
empowered me to finish this project (You know who you are);
and
to my editor and publisher, both "God-sends," who truly made this
a reality and to whom I will forever be in a debt of gratitude.
and last but not least,
to my illustrator, Patricia Gordon-Riveria, a native New Yorker
(Brooklyn), with a humble heart, a giving spirit and a wealth
of untapped talent. Her frequent words to me?..."Wow look
at God, I didn't even know I could draw like that!"

Introduction

Esther is a book that omits the name of God, yet His providence and intervention are intricately written between the lines. It is a timeless story retold in the rhythm and fun of rhyme.

It is ethnically diverse in that this traditionally Jewish story is retold with an African American flair by a lady we could easily refer to as "the religious Dr. Seuss."

It is a story for all ages about respect, honor and extreme courage. It is written in the cadence of rhyme in order to give a familiar story and its inherent lessons an escape from tedium.

I have attempted to leave no stone unturned in my efforts to use common vernacular to pull readers into a story that evidence God's desire and ability to step into time and space of human existence and make a difference.

I attempt to captivate readers in the story, its history, and its divine lessons, reminding all that God is a God of and for His people. Underlying every line is the hope that everyone reading this embraces Him, as I have, as my God and my Friend!

One

Once upon a time. . .

There once was a pompous king.
He knew he had everything!
In the third year of his reign,
In the citadel of Susa, his domain,
a banquet[2] he threw.
His nobles, officials and military leaders all came.

For a 180-days
his kingdom displayed
vast wealth and splendor and glory
And this is just the beginning
of this really spicy story.

Now when these 180 days were over
the king still was not done.
This king from the land of Susa
had acquired a reputation
as, well, a "boozer"
Sooo, for seven days and seven nights
he threw a smaller party
and it was outta sight!

At the end of the party that- 'went off'- without a hitch.
He summoned Queen Vashti in a feverous pitch.
He wanted to show off her beauty, for she was quite a sight,
but she refused to come to the King that night.
The reason she declined?
Well, she was having a party at the same time!
but no one really knows for sure.

No matter what, it was more than
the King's pride would tolerate or endure.

Queen Vashti

Even the King's court of men had plenty to say
that the Queen should refuse the King in such a big way.
All the men were distained,
they went quite insane
and to the King's chambers did bolt!
"Get rid of her!" they said, "Off with her head!"
or all our women may revolt!

So, the King listened to the bad advice of his men
and found very much to his chagrin
that he was all alone!

"Let's have a beauty contest! He'll pick a new Queen!"
"A virgin that's beautiful and fit for a King!"
127 provinces sent forth their women
but few were chosen,
the choicest of the choice given.

In the King's harem they stayed
and every day bathed.
In perfumed oils and amazing scents,
nothing was spared, especially not expense.

They went in the evening
and returned in the day
Till they each got a chance; it went on that way.
They went to see the King one at a time
until he had seen the entire line!

One maiden was fairer than fair
she embodied grace with beauty so rare.
Poise was her gift and favor she was shown.
Esther was the name by which she was known.
"Esther" her name had a ring;
now it was her time to go before the King.
In the tenth³ month of his seven-year reign,
she found grace, favor and the royal crown obtained!

So happy was the King, that he threw a great feast
for all his princes and servants.
From the greatest to the least,
giving lots of presents according to his state.
We know he liked to party, and it went on rather late.
The King's a party animal—no—a party beast.
He partied hearty at this extravaganza called, "Esther's Feast!"

While you must be getting tired of this story and its rhyme,
I suggest you take a break but don't be gone a real long time,
get a drink and a snack,
Hurry back with all the fix-ins',
cause this is the part where the plot thickens!

Two

The Plot Thickens. . .

Esther had a secret that no one really knew,
a hush, hush secret that she was a Jew!
She had a cousin who became her dad,
a cousin who made the wrong man mad.

Her cousin refused to bow to Haman,
the man who King Xerxes had made second in the land.
This made ole' Haman mad as could be.
So, he said,"Kill all the Jews," and "make it a decree!"
So, Mordecai (pronounced more-dah-kay-eye), Esther's cousin-dad,
ripped his clothes, wore sackcloth and ashes.
Oh my! was he sad!

To the palace he ran, to tell Esther his plight
and explain how he and all the Jews were in danger that night!
Esther listened and listened well.
She asked, "What can I do?" then her countenance fell.
"You can go to the king and plead for our lives!" he replied.
"Do something, you must, to turn this evil tide!"

Esther told her cousin-dad
that things were really rough,
She couldn't go before the king, unless called,
or death would result

"If you think you'll escape because you're in the King's palace,
or you think you'll escape because you drink from a chalice,
then your thinking is wrong, you're thinking amiss!
Who knows if you were brought to the kingdom-
-for such a time as this!"

So, then Esther said, "Let's go on a fast, you, I and all the Jews
and at the end of three days, I'll send you some news.
I'll fast and I'll pray, for my people I cherish
then I'll go before the King and if I perish, "I perish!"

In the meantime, with every day that passed
Haman's hatred of the Jews grew vast.
He was on his way to see the King
about a need to sanction his dastardly deed.
He had built a gallows fifty cubits high
on which to hang ole Mordecai!

As Haman relished thoughts of his (Mordecai) demise,
He sought the King—who sought him—to his surprise!
To ask of him this: "How do I honor a man?"
"Who could it be other than me?" Haman thought:
*"O what bliss that the King should do this
to none other than me, my heart tells me so..."*
and HATRED fell prey to EGO!

So, Haman walked in and said with a grin,
"Give him of your clothes and of your horse and of your crown
and let him be driven all around town;
that all may behold and see
how you honor "me"—I mean- your 'honoree'!"

Then said the King to Haman "make it so
and please, don't tell me no!"
"Do all that you said and leave nothing out!
Take my clothes, and my horse, and my crown
and pull this dear chap all over town."
"For he exposed a plot to take my life one day
an honorable deed that has not been repaid."
"So please, not one ounce of honor can I deny,
do this—for old man Mordecai!"

Haman left the King's presence abruptly.
for he knew he would soon throw uppidity, uppidity,
he was sick to his stomach as sick as could be.
"Honor old Mordecai over me!"

"How can I do this?" but do it I must
or the king will know me—he can't trust!
So, I'll just have to be on my P's and Q's
more determined than ever to eliminate the Jews!

Three

As the story goes. . .

Now the three days were over,
and the fasting had stopped.
It was time for Esther to face her lot.
So, into the inner court she went, to see the King
and there she found a funny thing.

The King extended his scepter of gold
and offered the Queen all her desire could hold
"Up to half my Kingdom I'd give,
just name what you want, whatever it is!"

"Oh nothing!" she exclaimed,
was the response of her lips,
"Just come to my banquet."
then she left with a twirl of her tiny little hips.

Off to the banquet they go—
the King, with Haman in tow.
And when they had wined and dined,
Once again said the King to the Queen
in their merrymaking,
"Half the Kingdom be thine for the taking!"

Now Haman knew Queen Esther was strange
or maybe she was just really deranged.
Who in their right mind would turn down a king,
a king who was offering half of everything!

What was on her mind, did she not have a clue?
Oh my, did he know exactly what he would do.
He'd take the wealth, half and more if he could,
he'd take it all! Yes, he sure would!

But once again she refused the kingdom and its riches.
She had more valuable things in mind,
things of virtue and freedom
things of the noble kind.

she asked once again
for them to attend
her banquet of wine.
She said, "I will be sure
to tell you <u>all</u> this time."

Now the second banquet was as good as the first,
the food and the wine were the best
and now was the time for Esther's request!

"If I have found favor in thy sight,
let my life be given me at my petition this night.
and to my people, I pray, give a reprieve
from this tangled web that Haman doth weave!"

Haman began to fear for his life,
'cause he could sense the King's growing strife.
He fell on the Queen's bed and began to beg
just when the king turned around his royal head.

"Will Haman force the Queen before me this night?!"
Was his wine clouded thought
as he saw the compromising sight.

Just as he made this erroneous assumption
there came a chamberlain with lots of gumption.
"It is finished! Behold the gallows, fifty cubits high,
which Haman built for Ole Mordecai!"
and the King said with little remorse,
"Take him and hang him on his own gallows, of course!"

Four

The Saga Continues. . .

So, they took him fast and they hung him high
a fate he deserved—"that"—no one can deny!
There Haman hung on the gallows he had built
but no one could seem to feel any guilt.

Not Mordecai who was set in charge
over Haman's 'house at Large.'
The King had given Mordecai Haman's ring
and told him to take the house and run everything.

Esther came forth and fell at the King's feet
and there she cried for the solution was incomplete.
"My people are destined for destruction
unless you, my King, get a serious unction,
to make Haman's wrong right,
and give all the Jews the chance to fight."

So, the King wrote a document to spell it all out
and just so there'd be no doubt.
He sealed it with his ring
which meant it had become an irrevocable thing.

They were given the right to bear arms,
to keep women and children free from all harm.
to take the spoils and take the plunder,
to conquer, divide and protect,
to cast fear asunder.

So, on the thirteenth day in the month of Adair,
in the countryside, in the city wide
the noise of war began to rise like thunder.
The Jews destroyed all their enemies
but didn't keep the plunder!

Sooo, the Jews smote their enemies
with the stroke of the sword,
"Your enemies will be your foot stool!"[4]
Thus saith the Lord.

Yes, they wiped out their enemies, even Haman's ten sons.
They hung on his gallows until there were none.
And many a hater changed as they heard the news,
they stopped hating and decided to become Jews.

Don't believe me? Read it for yourself.
It's right there in the book
chapter eight verse seventeen,
Go ahead, take a look!

So once again the first become last
and the last become the first[5]
and it's getting about time to end this verse.

By day fifteen, the victory was won.
A new celebration had finally begun.
O Nathan had cast lots for their ruin.
So, they called the celebration the days of Purim.

I should put this story to an end,
but there are so many lessons inherent within.
It was placed in the Great Book of Books,
so, it's worth us taking a closer look.

Five

I Heard it thru the Great Vine[1]

Lesson one is easy,
It shouldn't have to be said
listen to the king—or off with your head[6]
Yes, the meek shall inherit the earth someday[7]
until then – do it the "king's" way.
Keep his manner and temper mild
or he just might banish you to exile.
If you don't get what I mean
then take it from a modern-day queen
—Aretha—
the Queen of Soul!
It seems the key to all authority is R-E-S-P-E-C-T
I'm told.

Lesson Two is just for you,
A woman is not a thing or possession to be shown
but a person, to cherish, love and honor—not to own

Lesson Three
Watch what your friends tell you to do,
I'd check with God first, if I were you,
'cause friends will gripe and groan,
but in the end, you're the one all alone.
Check with God and forget all the rest.
We all know "Father (God) knows best!"

Lesson Four
Wine clouds the thinking' and blurs the mind,
dulls the perception and judgement most of the time.
No wonder the Bible says don't be filled with wine
but filled[8] with the Spirit
I know, I know, you don't want to hear it.

I know the Greek word for "filled" means "controlled by"
but let's be real, we all try.
We start out controlling the drink
but before we can think,
the tide turns in a rush
and the "drink" instead controls us!

Lesson Five
If you want to be a Queen
better "lock up" that "thing!"
I don't say that with malice,
But let the record show,
only virgins[9] were chosen to go to the palace!

Virginity alone may not make you rare
you still got to show that you really do care
'bout more than yourself,
'bout your community at large,
and trust God to lead and take charge.

Esther truly was rare indeed
She didn't just listen to her elders
But instead, she took heed

She was humble but not timid
She followed all the rules
But knew its limits.
She knew her predicament was odd
But in spite of it all, she chose to trust God.

And as a result, she became the orphan
Who saved a nation,
and believe it or not, all of creation
I'm not talking about just a few
I know you know Jesus was a Jew.

So, if the race wasn't saved
by this orphan's bold act
We'd all still be in sin and that's a fact.

Lesson Six-let's put fellas in the mix
So, fellas if you like what you see
take it from me,
remember first she's God's property!
Okay, don't take it from me, hard head!
You do the math,
mishandle God's property
and incur God's wrath!

Don't feel sorry,
Hey baby, Hey,
like what you see?
Here's some Beyonce' advice:
She floats your boat and keeps your fire lit?
So, all I'm saying is—- "PUT A RING ON IT!"[10]

Lesson Seven
This one is about Beauty within and without.
One needs them both without a doubt.
Some people have beauty naturally,
and others do their best to hone,
but make no mistake
"Beauty's only skin deep
but ugly is to the bone!"[11]

This brings us to Lesson Eight
Be careful of the ditch you've dug,
the plot you've wrote,
the web you've wove,
the seeds you've sown,
In the end, the demise may be your own!

Lesson Nine
It's not too late, the principle still holds,
you reap what you sow
but remember it may be your kids
that pay the debt that you owe.
The sins of the Father visit the children you know.[12]

Lesson eleven …but first ten and then the end
Lesson Ten
Let's not forget
These principles are not just for the sinister
You can reap what you sow
And become prime minister!

Mordecai refused to bow
not because it was hard
but he knew not to bend
to anyone but God

God's design is always grand
He's the man with the plan
He protects his people
Yes, his church and their steeple

So have hope in all that happens to you.
For God's got your back and he always come thru!

Lesson Eleven
Some days the battle's the Lord's
and some days you may have to fight.
No matter the occasion,
God's there to make it right.

No worries or regrets
God has never failed me yet
It may be so hard that you'll have to moan
Just remember, He takes care of his own

So, when circumstances seem strange
and your options seem limited,
don't dare give up cause God's still in it!
No matter where life finds you,
God won't leave you there without a prayer.
He will use you where you are
for your good and His Glory.
Don't believe me? Read Esther's story!

    —The End (for Esther…the beginning for You!)

All In His Hands

Endnotes

1   John 15:5 (NIV).

2   This was more like a county fair that lasted half a year. Also, according to Keil and Delitzsch, 1973, Vol. three, Esther p. 332-324, such a long feast may have been to accommodate the hosts of provinces officials and dignitaries with varying work schedules. More a fair than a banquet. The text says the King displayed his wealth that long not necessarily that the banquet lasted that long. It was long enough for the king to display the glory and riches of his kingdom. (Disney World's display is open year-round too)

3   Ten is the number of completion, universality, restoration, and God's authority. (For example, "God said" is used ten times in Genesis and his Word is reflected in Ten Commandments, His Divine authority). In scripture, seven symbolizes the number of perfection, totality, and completeness as well. Biblical numerology-10. http://numerology center. retrieved 3/15/2022.6 Mysterious Numbers in the Bible and What They Mean. (Dave Roos, July 22.2021), people.howstuffworks. com retrieved 3/15/2022. *Understanding Biblical numbers (2015).* http://www. harvestime.org. retrieved March 15, 2022.

4   Ps. 110:1;Luke 20:43(NIV).

5   Matt. 20:16 (NIV).

6   Prov. 20:2 (NIV).

7   Ps. 37:11;Matt.5:5(KJV).

8   Eph.5:18(NIV).
     Pieres being full complete, completely occupied with, controlled by, (4134,4137,4138), as found in Hebrew-Greek Key Word study Bible(NASB). (Chattnooga, TN: AMG Publishers), 2254. Enkrates (1468,) Strong's Concordance, (Grand Rapids, Michigan: Zondervan), 1604.

9   Esther 2:3 (KJV)

10   Single Ladies" Beyonce Knowles released October 8, 2008.

11   This maxim was first stated by Sir Thomas Overbury in his poem "A Wife" (1613): All the carnal beauty of my wife is but skin-deep". But according to Quote Investigator, in 1824, The *American Farmer* of Baltimore, MD published a piece by "A backwoodsman" about a fictional court case. "It is a trite saying that beauty is but skin deep, yet I have heard it said that ugly goes to the bone, and I am sure that there is nothing in this doctrine so beautiful as to prevent its penetrating even to the marrow." Dorothy Parker is attributed to have said this in 1977 but she died in 1967 and therefore this has not been supported. From http:// quoteinvestigator.com retrieved March 15, 2022.

12   Exodus 20:4-6. This verse states that father's sins (of those who hate God) will go to third and fourth generation and is the reason some believe in generational curses. But it should be noted that blessings are handed down generationally to thousands of generations to those who love him, and this author believes it should be coupled or considered with other scriptures.

Printed in the United States
by Baker & Taylor Publisher Services